EXPLORING
EXETER

THE QUAY

JEAN MAUN

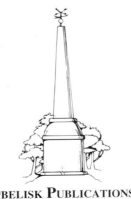

OBELISK PUBLICATIONS

ALSO IN THIS SERIES
Exploring Exeter – The West Quarter, *Jean Maun*
Exploring Exeter – The Heart of the City, *Jean Maun*

OTHER TITLES OF INTEREST
The Ghosts of Exeter, *Sally and Chips Barber*
The Lost City of Exeter – Revisited, *Chips Barber*
The Great Little Exeter Book, *Chips Barber*
Beautiful Exeter, *Chips Barber*
An Exeter Boyhood, *Frank Retter*
Around the Churches of Exeter, *Walter Jacobson*
Street-names of Exeter, *Mary Ruth Raymond*
Topsham Past and Present, *Chips Barber*
Topsham in Colour, *Chips Barber*
Pinhoe of Yesteryear, *Chips Barber*
Pinhoe of Yesteryear Part II, *Chips Barber*
Whipton of Yesteryear, *Chips Barber and Don Lashbrook*
Heavitree of Yesteryear, *Chips Barber*
Ide of Yesteryear, *Mavis Piller*
St Thomas of Yesteryear, *Mavis Piller*
St Thomas of Yesteryear Part II, *Mavis Piller*
Ian Jubb's Exeter Collection
An Alphington Album, *Pauline Aplin and Jeanne Gaskell*
Around & About the Haldon Hills – Revisited, *Chips Barber*
Murders and Mysteries in Devon, *Ann James*

We have over 180 Devon titles; for a current list please send SAE to
Obelisk Publications, 2 Church Hill, Pinhoe, Exeter EX4 9ER

Plate Acknowledgements
All pictures by Chips Barber
apart from pages 4 (top), 9 and 11 (top) supplied by Jean Maun
and page 19 (bottom) supplied by Mavis Piller.

First published in 2002 by
Obelisk Publications, 2 Church Hill, Pinhoe, Exeter, Devon
Designed and Typeset by Sally Barber
Printed in Great Britain
by Colour C Ltd, Tiverton, Devon

© Jean Maun/Obelisk Publications 2002

Exeter Quay

Exeter is a beautiful city. When I am asked which part of it I like most, the immediate reply is 'the Quay and the river'.

I prefer to approach Exeter Quay from the west bank of the river, and reach the opposite side by walking over the admirable Cricklepit footbridge. This blue metal bridge was designed by David Hubbard and opened on 29 June 1988 by Mayor O'Callaghan. On that day the pupils of Montgomery School dressed up in costumes of the times of previous bridges, and formed a procession over it.

The bridge leads towards the area where Cricklepit Mill was situated; it sadly burnt to the ground in June 1999. It is an ancient name, over the years corrupting from Crikenpette, circa 1185, to Crykepit Mills in 1599. By 1850, the narrow lane beneath the city wall had become known as Cricklepit Street, meaning 'the pit beneath the cliff'.

Although, from a distance, Cricklepit Bridge looks a somewhat flimsy structure, as we start walking over it we can see that this is not so – it is quite substantial!

Whilst facing the river, before crossing the bridge, pause to look up at the Exeter skyline. To the left, we see a group of red-brick buildings above the riverside development known as Shilhay; brick flats follow and then a group of poplars conceal one of the towers of the Cathedral.

A round tower is visible between two blocks of flats; this is the stair tower of the Cathedral and Quay multi-storey car park. The area was excavated in 1990, prior to the construction of the car park, and archaeologists found remains of buildings belonging to a formerly unknown Roman fort, or military compound. Occupying about four acres and overlooking the river, this site would have commanded excellent views over the early fording place of the Exe, very close to the point where the two Exe Bridges are now to be found. The city wall runs down through the middle of the site, which may pre-date the main legionary fortress discovered in 1971 on the Cathedral Green. It may have been a base for the main fort, or a satellite fort. Not only did it include the remains of buildings, but also evidence of a road, a gateway, trenches and ditches. Early Roman pottery was found, some of which may well have been made in Exeter.

Further around to the right is a red-brick gabled building with a white cygnet drawn out on the apex, underneath which appear the words 'New Theatre'. This building was erected in 1913 in Friars Gate and was the Holy Trinity Church Hall, belonging to a church in South Street. It became redundant when the church closed in 1969. For a while St Leonard's Church leased it to the International School in Wonford Road as a recreational centre. After extensive renovation and some extensions, it is now used by the Cygnet Theatre, a training school for aspiring young thespians.

To the right and forward a little, there is a red-brick tower about the same height as the theatre. This is the top of the façade of the Salvation Army Temple, on the corner of Friars Gate and Friars Walk, used by the Salvationists for over a century. The site has religious connections which go back to the 1300s. Before then the Greyfriars dwelt in very unsanitary conditions in the Bartholomew Street area, from where bad smells often wafted over the city. When King Edward I visited Exeter in 1284, in order to resolve the Walter Lechlade murder, the Bishop promised the King that he would find better accommodation for the monks. The Friars moved to this area in 1303 and built a priory, hence the names of the streets. At the dissolution of the monasteries, the area fell into disrepair. It became the property of the Colleton family in the early nineteenth century.

The site was sold to the Quakers in 1832; they built a meeting place to replace the one in Wynards Lane, which would no longer accommodate their increased numbers. The building was designed to hold 700 people, but proved to be too ambitious, so they built another one on their Wynards Lane site and returned there. The hall was sold to the Temperance movement; in 1872 it was hired by the Exeter School Board, to be used as a junior and infant school until the Holloway Street school was built in 1876. (The latter was St Nicholas School for many years, but is now the home of the Jehovah's Witnesses.) The original octagonal hall remains part of the Temple; its Georgian façade can easily be picked out in contrast to the elaborate Victorian extensions. Complete with towers either side, the river front was added in 1889, seven years after William Booth bought the hall. The towers were later removed.

Colleton Villa, once known as Colleton House, is the large white house that can be seen in front of the previously mentioned buildings. The villa was built in 1820 as the Colleton family home; they commissioned Matthew Nosworthy, who built Colleton Crescent, to construct it. It is a well-proportioned house, built in the classical style and set in beautiful gardens. When the city was bombed on 4 May 1942, the Exeter County Court offices were destroyed by fire. A few days later, Colleton Villa was requisitioned for the use of the County Court offices, where they remained until 1961. The building is still used as offices.

There are three other white, rendered houses between this and the theatre. Lawn House and Magnolia House stand on the site of the old priory and were just one house when built in the eighteenth century. Two massive doors used in Magnolia House may once have belonged to the monastery. In the 1950s, when Lawn House underwent repairs, steps were discovered under the ground floor, which were thought to have led to a passage giving access to the river. The third white house is the equally attractive Acacia House.

To the right of Colleton Villa is a large white block of uninspiring flats named Riverside Court. It was designed by David Saxon of Bristol, and built in 1973 on the site of an early Victorian house.

I really love the name of one of the nearby streets: Lucky Lane. I have seen it named Graves Street on an old map; when some of the houses were built, skeletons were discovered, so perhaps this was the area of the last resting places of the friars. On an even older but undated map, I have also seen this area referred to as Friars Hay.

If you stop in the middle of Cricklepit Bridge and look either side, the views are most attractive. To the left is a panoramic view upriver to the twin Exe Bridges. On the west bank is a former malt house, which has been converted into a public house by Brewer's

Fayre. Nearer to us is a large eight-acre development of over one hundred cream-coloured apartments with a continental style piazza and riverside walk. The land covered by this property was the site of the last industrial premises on the Port of Exeter. Until the early 1970s, there was a small oil refinery supplied by tankers such as *Ben Johnson* and the *Esso Jersey*.

Commenced in 1988, the Haven Banks scheme was an award-winning design by Halliday and Meecham. When the plans were put out to tender, the council made the stipulation that the complex should be in sympathy with the warehouses on the Quay, and not any higher. A small shop is situated on the ground floor at the end of each block,

and between the first and second blocks is an iron arch under which are attractive gates leading to the central piazza.This is for the private use of residents.

Opposite these buildings, on the east bank, is the development known as Shilhay, with its wide grassy bank sweeping down from the houses to the water's edge. In the 1970s, the Shilhay was cleared of its warehouses and small factories and developed as a housing estate by Warren and Taylor. It now has the appearance of a lovely riverside village. The tasteful design of flats and houses of varying heights and widths, arranged at attractive angles around irregular-shaped courtyards, brought the architects accolades and rewards. Because the woollen trade was once a vital industry here, the courtyards and walkways are

named after the processes used in the trade: Dyers Court, Fullers Court, Tuckers Court and so on. Even the nearby pub, the Bishop Blaize, is named after the patron saint of the woollen trade. The odd one out is Gabriel Court, a reminder that there used to be a wharf of that name here.

To our right is a stunning view of the Quay. If we continue to walk to the other end of the bridge, we will see directly in front of us, two bonded warehouses. These were constructed on the site of an old coal quay. The first one was built for Kennaway and Company in 1892. Founded in 1743 by William Kennaway, the firm was involved in the woollen trade; when that industry declined, it turned to importing wine. Exonians may recall seeing wine barrels lined up outside their premises in nearby Palace Gate. (This city centre property remained in the Kennaway family until 1975, when it was taken over by the South Street Baptist Church. If you look carefully at the windows, you will see a design of vines painted on the glass around the edges reminding us of its former use.) The quayside warehouse, consisting of two storeys, appears to be in three sections, each of which has a dark, tiled, gabled roof.

It is obvious that the two parts on the right have been refurbished, as there is now a new grey balcony along the front of the second floor; tables and chairs are placed on it for the benefit of its patrons.

The second warehouse has a totally different appearance as it is built of a beige-coloured stone and has shuttered windows on both of its floors.

To get a better look at the front of these two buildings, take the footpath ahead which leads to Commercial Road. One has a wide glass door outlined with black, which looks very modern. Above this is a sign which says 'Bonded Warehouse', under which is its present name 'Mud Dock'.

On the opposite side of the road is a new development of six apartments called 'Leat Side', some of which have small shops underneath. Nearby is the small stone Quay Bridge that dates from 1681, and is the oldest bridge on the Quay. It has two arches spanning the higher and lower leats. The higher leat, the right stream of the two, comes off the Exe about a mile upstream at The Mill on the Exe, a former paper mill which has been converted into a public house.

> THIS BONDED CELLAR WAS
> ERECTED BY SAMUEL JONES
> OF THIS CITY. WINE MERCHANT
> AND ONE OF THE REPRESENTATIVES
> IN THE TOWN COUNCIL
> FOR S⁺ DAVID'S WARD. AND THIS
> CORNER STONE WAS LAID BY EMILY
> HIS WIFE. ON THE 4ᵗ FEBRUARY 1878,
> SHERIFF OF EXETER NOVEMBER 1880
> MAYOR —— ᴅᴏ —— ᴅᴏ —— 1883

These medieval man-made watercourses passed under the mills to drive the mill wheels of this lowland part of the city. Extracted from a point upstream, the water drove as many as 25 waterwheels at one time. This area was the medieval industrial heart of Exeter, and it was here that the finishing of the woollen cloth took place. The bridge was built to enable people in the woollen industry to bring their cloth to the Quay for transportation to the continent, and to give access to the rack fields. These consisted of many small fields covered with wooden racks and fitted with the tenter hooks on which the woollen cloth was stretched to dry. These gave rise to the saying that people were on 'tenterhooks' or stretched to their limit. By the bridge, the two leats join and run as one towards the river.

After crossing Quay Bridge we reach The Quay, one of the most pleasant and interesting areas of Exeter. The oldest buildings date from 1680, when the Port was re-organised, the quay enlarged to twice its length, and the canal lengthened and improved.

Walking forward a little from the bridge, we turn left and find ourselves facing the red-brick Custom House, a substantial building which has undergone renovation. This is the oldest surviving Custom House in England; the architect was Richard Allen, and it cost £3,000 to build. The earliest settlement in Exeter occurred at this point. It was near the tidal limit of navigation so a stone quay was built and a route cut through the rocky cliffs above.

Exeter had a flourishing woollen trade from the twelfth to the eighteenth century, and the building of the Custom House in 1681 gave the city rights over Topsham. The latter had been the principal port of the river Exe ever since the Earls of Devon made weirs across the river in the thirteenth century. The Courtenays owned most of the land around the river estuary, including the port of Topsham, so this deed ensured that they received all the dues on goods landed there. We'll hear more of this later.

Take a close look at the Custom House and notice that the five arches surrounding the door and ground floor windows seem an odd feature. Originally there was an open arcade so that the goods, which had just been unloaded onto the Quay, could easily be brought to shelter. When Celia Fiennes visited the city in 1698, she described the Custom House in great detail, noting its 'open space below with rows of pillars, which they lay in goods just as they are loaded off the ships in case of wet'. She did, however, omit to mention the Queen's Pipe, a great stove installed on the ground floor for burning off contraband goods. The arches on the right were filled in during 1685 to make an office for the Customs Officer, and the others were enclosed in the eighteenth century to provide more storage, which was desperately needed in order to carry out the duties within the building. The Port of Exeter had responsibility for all ports from Teignmouth to Lyme Regis. Officers had to be vigilant as they not only had to watch for illicit goods being landed on or near the Quay, but also had to chase the local smugglers around the narrow lanes of the area. On the first floor above these arches are five long windows belonging to the upper rooms.

The three flights of the massive staircase and a gallery form a rectangular hall inside. Celia Fiennes described her ascent up the handsome stairs into a large room full of desks and little partitions for the writers and accountants, saying it was 'full of books and files of paper'. The handrail of the stairs is nearly as wide as the newel cap. The most stunning part of the building is the Long Room upstairs, which she described. The Baroque plaster ceiling includes curving oak branches with leaves, acorns, animals, flowers and fruits, built over sticks and scrim and therefore hanging. It is the work of the famous plasterer John Abbot of Frithelstock (1639–1727). Some of the rooms on this floor provided accommodation for the Customs officers. There are also less extravagant ceilings over the staircase and in the Surveyor's room. According to an illustrated book of the Abbot family's work, the whole lot cost £35. There are other ceilings resembling these at Bideford and Youlston Park in North Devon.

The Custom House used to have a collection of spits. Now to be found in nearby Quay House, these long, sharp, steel instruments with a hollowed-out channel on one side were used by the custom officer to check that illicit goods were not hidden in a cargo. The expression 'not to trust further than one can spit' is derived from the functions of these instruments.

A two-bay extension on the right was built in the eighteenth century. Replacement Georgian sash windows are now to be seen on the façade, but if you take a walk around the back of the building, you will see the original leaded transom and mullioned windows. It is said that this is the oldest surviving all-brick building in Exeter, although the partly brick-built Tudor House in Tudor Street also dates from the seventeenth century.

HM Customs & Excise vacated the premises in September 1989 after a continuous occupation that spanned 308 years. The building was externally restored in 1992. It has a hipped roof with a pediment in the middle on which is the Royal Coat of Arms of George IV, dated 1820. This was restored in 1988.

Take a walk along the path between the leats and the antique shop situated on the left of the Custom House, and you can see a very high wall with a large arch, which is now completely filled in. At one time, but no longer, it was thought that this might have been where the Water Gate was situated. To the left of this arch, just above the top of it, is another small arch, which is believed to have provided an outlet for the Coombe Brook. This stream rose in the Bishop's Palace gardens, flowed through Coombe Street and down to the river. Because it posed problems, it was piped; there is now no evidence, apart from a dip in the ground, that it ever existed.

Walk across the back of the Custom House and look up to see the city wall. The break where the area is grassed and planted with flowers was caused when a section of the wall fell on the Custom House Inn in 1927. To the left of this is where the Water Gate was more likely situated. This was the fifth of the city's gates and was built in 1566, when the new canal re-opened the Port of Exeter to shipping. A porter was appointed to lock the gate at dusk and take the key to the mayor. The gate was demolished in 1815.

The two cannons in front of the Custom House were part of a consignment of sixteen manufactured in Scotland for the Imperial Russian Army for use against the French during the Napoleonic Wars, but they were never collected nor delivered. Originally, four of them were intended to be placed by the Wellington Monument in Somerset. However, on arrival at Exeter, they were impounded to cover import duties. When it was discovered that they were not from the Battle of Waterloo, they were no longer required and so remained at Exeter, some lying in a store, others used as bollards along the Quay. However, if you take a trip to the Wellington Monument, at least one of them can be seen pointing over the town. When the Quay was redesigned in 1983, these two were restored and mounted on gun carriages.

There are further buildings attached to the left of the Custom House. One looks like a warehouse; it houses the Exeter Crafts Guild on the lower floor and antiques on the upper one, reached by a flight of exterior stone steps.

The building between this and the Custom House used to be called Singers Café. You are able to walk around one and then go through to the other as they are linked. The café obtained its name from the fact that the tabletops are fixed on the bases of old treadles of Singer sewing machines, but it has changed hands and is now labelled 'Craft Centre'.

There is a feature outside based on an armillary sphere, an ancient astronomical instrument which shows the main divisions of the heavens and the movement of celestial bodies. It is a large hemisphere with a flat circular plane, inclined at an angle of 33 degrees. A number of semi-circles, representing the meridian, equator, horizon, tropics and so on, are around it rising upwards above the

plane. This one has a ring representing the meridian going from either side to the top marked out in angles like a surveyor's theodolite, 90 degrees being at the top. One of the semi-circles around it has the following signs of the zodiac sculptured on it: two fish for Pisces; the ram for Aries; the bull for Taurus; the twins for Gemini; the crab of Cancer; and last of all, the lion for Leo. The plane surface is not completely flat as it has a globe sculptured in the middle representing the earth, with a pole going up from its middle to the 90 degrees on the meridian. All around it is an area representing the ocean; it features crabs, star fish, lobsters and other sea creatures.

On the outer part the surface is divided into twelve and labelled with the months of the year. It looks as if it is made of bronze, but I noticed that one of the rings was broken and that it is actually constructed of wood painted to represent metal. It was sculptured by Roger Dean and placed there in 1990 to the memory of Sylvia Bull. The original armillary sphere probably dates back to about 255BC.

Passing in front of the Custom House, we cross the bottom of Quay Hill. A stone warehouse on our left has been converted into a night club called Volts.

Next to this is a charming little red-brick building with a Dutch gable bearing the City's Coat of Arms. This is the Wharfinger's house, built in 1778 when Exeter was a thriving port. The Wharfinger was responsible for the loading and unloading of goods, and controlling the traffic on the river and canal – a kind of waterway traffic warden. If you saw the BBC Television series *The*

Onedin Line, this was the house used as the Chandler's shop. Now it is occupied by Age Concern.

Next to the Wharfinger's House is Quay House, a seventeenth-century warehouse, the oldest in Britain by a hundred years. However, there is a warehouse in Rockport, Massachusetts, USA, which equals this one in age. Quay House was built in 1680 as a transit shed for woollen cloth and other goods. It was built on the site of an older warehouse, called the Crane Cellar because a crane stood near it. Before the Crane Cellar was built, from time immemorial goods had been landed onto a natural shelf of hard red rock, which was exposed at this spot.

Looking at Quay House, you can see that the top of the front overhangs the pavement, and is supported by massive dark brown wooden beams. When it was built, the river was much wider and water ran in front of the warehouse underneath this overhang. Small boats could moor, load and unload in the dry. Until the late 1980s it was a DIY timber store, but it was fully restored in 1987 by the Exeter Canal and Quay Trust, who opened it as an interpretation centre and small museum. On the ground floor there are lively displays and illustrations explaining the development of the Port of Exeter from Tudor times, by means of a mixture of prints, paintings, and objects such as barrels, bales of woollen cloth and tillet blocks. These were wooden blocks engraved with the coats of arms of the towns that sent woollen cloth to Exeter to be finished and exported. They were used to stamp the material covering the bales of cloth to show the town of origin. Upstairs, where export goods were once stored, the original pine timbers can be seen supporting the roof. This area now resembles a small cinema and houses an audio-visual presentation 'A Celebration of Exeter', which describes the history of the city. This free presentation lasts about fifteen minutes and is well worth seeing.

When excavating in 1985, archaeologists found a Tudor dock made of Heavitree stone in front, which can still be seen below pavement level. It dates from 1566, when the first pound-lock canal in the country, the Exeter lighter canal, was built. The dock had been filled in by 1700 to allow sea-going ships to reach the Quay and tie up there.

Nearby is the Prospect Inn. This formed part of Quay House 200 years ago, and the continuous roofs of the two verify this fact. It became an inn in 1830, and was originally called The Fountain. In 1955 the *Daily Sketch* bought it, renovated it, and offered it as a prize in their newspaper. Diana Dors made the presentation, but sadly the winner went bankrupt within two years.

On the right, in front, the nineteenth-century rectangular part was called Rose Cottage, and was the house of the ferryman. It was incorporated into the inn in 1965. It is of varying heights as it follows the contours of the hill behind, and of Prospect Steps beside it. These steps lead up to Colleton Crescent.

Next to the Prospect is a sight you might recognise if you watched *The Onedin Line* in the 1970s. This location was used in the quayside scenes to depict the Port of Liverpool

as it was in the early 1860s. In 1971, a three-masted schooner, the *Charlotte Rhodes*, came up to the Quay and tied up there several times. There was great excitement in Exeter and people often made a bee-line for the river to view the filming. For many weeks my husband, who taught at the John Stocker Secondary Modern Boys School, took sandwiches for lunch and ate them on the Quay whilst watching the 'action'. This was permitted as long as everyone kept very quiet.

It is a good job the buildings below are handsome, as they dwarf the seventeenth-century warehouse near them. The first of the two was built in 1834 of grey Pocombe stone with the corners and windows outlined in red bricks. In 1835, the Hooper family built the second in red Heavitree sandstone. The need for more warehouse accommodation was evident in 1827, after the final enlargement of the canal led to greater imports.

If you look at the tops of these buildings, you can still see the pulleys used for raising the goods into the loading bays, which still form the openings of the top floors. The windows, which are on each side of the bays, have heavy iron bars. This was because these were bonded warehouses used for storing tobacco, wine and other commodities on which duty had not been paid. The goods would then have been redistributed to various towns all over the country.

In more recent times, these warehouses were used by small private firms; On The Waterfront, a public house, was created on the ground floor. The warehouses were refurbished in 1989 at a cost of £2m, and a lift was put between the two to allow access; being listed buildings, the fronts could not be altered. They now contain offices, and there are small businesses on their ground floors. Next to these are the public conveniences!

Further along the Quay, there is a long, high brick wall, with twelve large, curved doors in it. These are the entrances to brick-lined cellars extending some 60 feet into the base of the cliff. They were once used for storing anything from cider to silk, on which duty had been paid. A local soap and candle manufacturer also used them and, during the Second World War, one was used as an air raid shelter. The BBC requisitioned another to use as an emergency transmitting station, if needed, while the local Royal Observer Corps used yet another.

After the war they housed small businesses. The street directory for 1965 reveals that Herbie Plain, motor cycle engineer; the Quay Printing Works; V. Kermond, motor engineer; and A. Sanford, firewood merchant, were just some of the traders operating here. After many years, these businesses were re-located to other premises whilst some ceased trading.

The cellars were re-developed to accommodate different small businesses, mostly of a craft nature. You will find shops for bicycle and tandem hire, antique lighting, wood furniture, and Exeter Swan crystal among others. Above these, about fifteen feet from the top of the cliff, there is a walkway hidden by ivy. This is where the excisemen used

to keep a look-out for any illicit goods coming into the port. These cellars are numbered from 13 to 24, the numbers up to 12 being the warehouses. There have been stories told of a secret tunnel from one of the cellars to a house on the top of the hill. The top entrance was said to have been discovered when Lawn House, mentioned on page 4, was restored in the 1950s.

The headquarters of the Sea Scouts is next along the Quay. Constructed of granite, this was built by the developers of the nearby flats; the Sea Scouts' old tin hut had to be demolished when the new building took place.

The first block of flats looks like a cream-coloured house. A large four-storey block called Clipper Quay follows, then another block of cream apartments, before we reach a group of grey, low flats. Like the apartments on Haven Banks, these are low to be in keeping with the area.

Now we will retrace our steps along the Quay. Opposite the warehouses, standing either side of the ferry crossing point, are two striking Gothic street lamps, made by Macfarlanes of Glasgow. These tall lamp-posts were placed here in 1983. Along with four others, they were originally made for the 1905 Exe Bridge; they were removed when the old bridge was demolished in 1973. They are painted green for a reason: this is the City's official colour. They also display the City's coat of arms.

There has been a ferry crossing point here since at least 1640. It is now called Butt's Ferry, after George Butt; he fought hard to save the service when the City Council considered it too costly to maintain. In the 1970s, the Department of the Environment ordered an enquiry when the Council approached the Government to obtain an Act of Parliament to have it closed. There was a public outcry. In 1978, the former Maritime

'TIS YER YOU
CATCH THE FERRY
A FUNNY BOAT IT
BE
BUT IT GETS
YOU ACROSS THE
RIVER
FOR ONLY 20P
CHILD 10P

Museum took over its running; at that time they had premises on both sides of the river. However, the ferry was constantly under threat after the Maritime Museum centred its entire activities at the Canal Basin. Some argued that when Cricklepit Bridge was built there would be no need for the ferry. It faced further problems: in 1989 it sank. With the odds heavily stacked against its survival, it was rescued by a city grant of £900. A purpose-built replacement ferry arrived in 1991, and the old one was moved by the Maritime Museum to the Basin, to connect its buildings on either side of the canal basin.

Now operating in summertime only, the ferry is a barge-like boat with rails for passengers to hold on to. The ferryman uses his hands to pull it along a waist-high wire, thereby propelling the boat across the river. There are, I believe, only two others like it in England.

A little beyond the ferry, a larger boat appears in the season. This is the *Southern Comfort*, which operates canal cruises to

Double Locks and Turf hotels. The boat has to pass over the ferry line, which the ferryman must drop each time it comes in or out.

There are also miscellaneous rowing boats and canoes for hire here, which people can take up the river or canal. The scene is one of intense activity on a fine summer's day or evening.

Opposite the Prospect Inn is a transit shed, supported by twelve cast iron pillars; it was built by Bodley Brothers, who owned a nearby foundry. This long open structure was used to provide undercover storage for cargo being transferred to the Quay from sea-going vessels. It was restored to its original condition in 1988. The former Maritime

Museum used to keep the Bedford lifeboat here. This oak-timbered and planked boat, presented to the museum by the Tyne Lifeboat Society, was used at Tynemouth, and was rowed by twelve men. In its 44 years of working life, which commenced in 1886, it went on 45 rescue missions, about one a year; its crew saved many lives along the north-east coast of England. In 1929, it was given a motor, but the following year it was taken out of commission.

Made of cast iron by Bodleys, there is also a contraption here called the King's Beam. This was used to support the custom man's scales; two men could work with a set of scales supported on either side. There are similar structures at Topsham and Dartmouth.

Bodleys used to manufacture a black stove, which was to be found in many West Country kitchens in the days before gas and electric ovens became more popular.

Beside the transit shed is a long building which used to be the fish market. It is now the Quay Antiques Centre, a popular place with those seeking to buy something unusual.

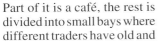

Part of it is a café, the rest is divided into small bays where different traders have old and odd items for sale: antiques, ephemera and bric-a-brac. I haven't found any treasures yet, but who knows!

Facing the river at the rear of this building is an open area with tables and chairs.

The Mallison Bridge spans the leat; opened on 19 September 1984 by his son, it was provided from the bequest of Harold Vincent Mallison, for the benefit of the public. This leads us back to Cricklepit Bridge.

The fun way to cross to the other side of the Exe is by Butts Ferry; the journey lasts a few minutes. We turn left and walk around the corner to find ourselves in an open area called Piazza Terracina, after Exeter's twin town in Italy.

First take the opportunity to pause here and look at the skyline across the river. To the right of Colleton Villa, and the flats previously mentioned, are the very attractive houses of Colleton Crescent, which, like Colleton Villa, was built by Matthew Nosworthy in the 1800s. At each end of the terrace are three-storey houses, and between them are four-storey houses with double-arched windows on the ground floor, typical of Nosworthy's style. They are all built of red brick with white string courses separating each floor, and white around the windows, which are sash shaped. On the ground floor these surrounds are made of Coade Stone, an artificial stone made up of secret ingredients. These were mixed, put into moulds and left to set, making a very hard-wearing building material. Examples of this stone can be found all over England, but the formula for the mixture remained a secret until the 1970s. George Coade was a wealthy resident of Exeter who went bankrupt and moved his family to London. His daughter, Eleanor Coade, jointly owned the London factory which made the stone, with Daniel Pincott. On Pincott's death, Eleanor became the sole owner of the factory, which continued to make the stone.

The central five houses of Colleton Crescent are stepped forward a little and are higher than the rest. The crescent is named after John Colleton, an Exeter merchant who, in 1737, first introduced a species of magnolia into England from Carolina. It is believed that the first one was brought to Exmouth; hence that town's main shopping precinct is the Magnolia Centre. Colleton's granddaughter, Louisa, laid the foundation stone of this group of houses in 1802; they were completed in 1814.

Most of the Victorian houses of Colleton and Southernhay were owned by the families of serving or retired naval and military officers and civil servants wishing to retire to the pleasant city of Exeter. There would also have been wealthy newcomers – professionals and businessmen – occupying these 'prestigious' properties. Now they accommodate businesses and a school of dancing, and some are divided into flats. At one time the Exeter Little Theatre Company occupied No 4, but they have since transferred to Preston Street in the West Quarter.

In 1971, Colleton Crescent was used as the houses of the gentry when *The Onedin Line* was being shot. Scenes from a film version of the *Hound of the Baskervilles* were also shot here, this becoming 221b Baker Street, the home of Sherlock Holmes.

In front of these elegant houses, grassy lawns sweep down to the wall above the cellars. On the railed edge of this cliff, green bushes hide the excisemen's former path: from these heights there is a fine view downriver!

PIAZZA TERRACINA

Meanwhile, back at the Piazza Terracina, we see to our right a row of shops built on the ground floor of the apartment blocks. Looking ahead, there is a huge three-storey red-brick building, which almost covers one side of the square. This was once a coal-fired power station, dating back to 1905. Its purpose was to provide electricity for the city's electric trams. It is a vast building and, for many years, was used by the Maritime Museum as a repair shop.

Exeter Corporation Electricity Station.

On the left of this square, with warehouses on either side of it, is the end of the Canal Basin. For the best part of three decades, until it closed in the 1990s, the Maritime Museum was a major tourist attraction; it boasted the world's biggest collection of boats, ranging in size from the tiniest of craft, housed in the various warehouses, to much larger ones lining the perimeter of the Basin. These 'assets' have been relocated to places like Bristol and Lowestoft.

This area has seen much residential development in recent years, and Maritime Court overlooks the Basin.

Just by the Basin is an unusual feature. It consists of a fairly large, round sunken area, which has wooden seats built all around the circumference. This is the remains of an old railway turntable, originally built to take Brunel's broad gauge track. The lines later

reverted to the more popular standard gauge. Both tracks can be identified, but Brunel's appear to be of a lighter metal. This was the goods link with the main line a few hundred yards away. The Great Western Railway used the broad gauge rails whilst the London and South Western Railway had the inner rails added to accommodate their standard gauge rolling stock.

THIS TURNTABLE, ONE OF TWO SERVING THE CANAL BASIN, WAS CONSTRUCTED TO CARRY STANDARD AND BROAD GAUGE TRUCKS. THE SITE WAS EXCAVATED AND MADE A FEATURE OF BY THE EXETER CITY COUNCIL TO CELEBRATE GWR 150. 24 SEPTEMBER 1985

We now continue with the river Exe to our left and the City Basin to the right where we pass warehouses; they must have been bonded as they have iron bars at their windows. After these are passed, very little can be seen on the right because a high grey stone wall obscures all. Nearly at the end of it, is a large blue corrugated iron shed with two doors. After this is a wide gap where workmen can put their cars while they labour on their boats. This is a good place to stop and have a look around again.

Gazing across the river we can see clearly the bottom of Colleton Hill and St Leonard's Quay. Ballast was once stored in a large recess under the cliff at the bottom of the hill, ready for the boats about to go to sea. There is a small blocked-in arch visible in the retaining wall by the river at the bottom of Colleton Hill. This is where the Shit Brook used to empty into the Exe. Before a sewerage system was engineered, all waste materials and effluent would make their way to the river via open brooks, and this name is indicative of the nature of the contents of this former stream. This foul watercourse was put underground following a cholera outbreak in 1832, which claimed the lives of several hundred citizens. Beyond the shed, the wall continues and we reach a point where the river is met by the canal at the King's Arms sluice.

Look across the river again to see the Port Royal Inn, a long, low, dark brown building and one of the longest pubs in England. It was originally a warehouse and later a row of cottages. It was reported in the *Illustrated London News* for 14 September 1850 that a mighty whirlwind on the Exe lifted boats off the river and over these cottages, depositing the boats on the fields rising behind them. It became a public house in the mid-nineteenth century. For many years, the single-storey part on the right was the headquarters of the

Exeter Rowing Club. They later moved to a site behind the former Maritime Museum. From here we can also see the lip of the flood relief channel and the suspension bridge further downriver.

When the waters of the Exe are high and flowing fast, the sluice gates of the King's Arms sluice are closed to prevent river water from entering the canal. There is a narrow wooden swing-bridge near the gates, which allows people to cross over the canal. Looking at the sluice, we can see to our right another bridge, which goes over the place where the canal meets the basin.

If the King's Arms sluice gates are open, we can cross the canal. Further to the right are the huge gasometers, which once used coal from Newcastle to produce gas for the city. They are no longer in use, but the area around them has been developed as offices for Transco, the gas company. There are also repair workshops for the fire service here. The headquarters of the Sea Cadets are along here; they are made of the same stone as the Sea Scouts' building.

A little further on, on the western side of the Exeter Canal, is the very attractive white-painted Welcome Inn, one of the first places in Exeter to be lit by gas. Rumour has it that, as at the famous Warren House Inn on Dartmoor, in the last century the fire never went out, but they never seemed to buy any coal.

I have heard that there is a bat colony near the pub. Also a species of jellyfish, said to be the smallest in England, can be found at this point in the canal.

It is probable that as early as the Roman times, rowing boats were able to reach Exeter, but the Exe was only navigable for larger boats as far as Topsham.

River traffic came to an end in 1284 when Isabella de Fortibus, Countess of Devon, built two barriers, or weirs, across the river at Countess Wear, leaving a gap of 30 feet between them. This made it impossible for anything other than the smallest boats to pass up to the city's quay.

In 1262, the male line of the Redvers, the Earls of Devon, had died out. The Earldom passed to Isabella, sister of the last Earl Baldwin, and widow of William de Fortibus. They were a rich and powerful family, with great influence and marriage connections to royalty, and the city of Exeter had continually to defend its commercial interests against successive earls. The family owned strategic lands and mills along the river, including the Port of Topsham. They must have realised that with every boat going to the city, a lot of duties were just sailing past their port to be unloaded upstream. The weirs were Isabella's solution to the family problem. She died in 1293, and in 1311 her heir Hugh de Courtenay, although not yet the Earl of Devon, took it upon himself to close the gap between the weirs, which had a disastrous effect on the city's trade. The problem seemed insoluble.

The earldom was adjudged to Hugh de Courtenay in 1335; the Courtenays were well and truly entrenched as the Earls of Devon. In 1461 Thomas Courtenay fell foul of the King and was beheaded. This seemed an opportune time for Exeter to petition to have the weirs moved; the citizens had always maintained that the waters of the Exe, from Exmouth to Cowley Bridge, ought to be common to the inhabitants to fish in and to have access to with their boats, vessels, ships and merchandise. On these grounds a document was prepared and sent to the relevant authorities, but no reply was given and nothing changed.

The decades passed and the woollen trade grew, becoming the chief industry of Exeter and its district, but all exported cloth had to be taken to Topsham as there was no other suitable outlet to the east or west of the city. However, in 1539, Henry Courtenay, once a great favourite of the King, was beheaded for treason. The city subsequently gained permission to start work to make the river navigable once more. But the intervening centuries had seen the Exe silt up behind the weir. To by-pass this obstacle, the decision was made to construct a canal.

Work began in 1545 and the churches of the city contributed towards the great cost of the project by donating part of their silver plate. The sale realised £229, but the work was delayed by the siege of Exeter during the Prayer Book Revolt in 1549.

In 1563 the work was recommenced with vigour, under John Trew of Glamorgan, but the end result was not entirely satisfactory. The canal was completed and vessels of up to ten tons could now, in theory, reach Exeter. However, complaints were frequently made that even smaller vessels could not come up at all states of the tide.

The canal, which was three feet deep and sixteen feet wide, started at the King's Arms sluice and followed a similar course to the present one, to a point where the Matford Brook joined the Exe.

Trew built a weir (Trew's Weir) across the river to control the height of the water in it. In this first canal there were three pairs of lock gates making pools so that lighters

could pass each other, and there was also a pair of gates at the southern end to retain the water at low tide. At the same time, a new quay, as mentioned earlier, was constructed under the city walls. As yet there was no City Basin and all vessels went directly from the canal and river to the Quay.

The canal opened in 1566; small boats could once more reach Exeter. Goods were unloaded from large ships anchored in the Exe estuary off Topsham, and then taken upriver by a fleet of lighters. It was not such a success as was hoped: boats could only enter the river at high tide, and silting was a problem.

The canal was closed several times for many days to effect repairs. During the English Civil War (1642–46) the banks were broken down as galloping horses were ridden along them. Further extensive repairs were effected in 1663.

George Browning built a fulling mill on the riverbank below Trew's Weir and had a leat constructed from above the weir. This was 58 feet wide and rejoined the river below the mill. It damaged the riverbank and the weir, and caused the canal to be closed for a month through a shortage of water. Barges were grounded, traffic delayed, but despite all this commercial inconvenience it still took a staggering seven years of litigation to close the mill. Although the council won their case, they had to be vigilant because Browning continued to attempt to work it for the next twenty years, in spite of the court's ruling!

Further improvements were made in 1671. The canal was again dredged and extended towards Topsham by cutting through the edge of Exminster marshes. Here there was a single pair of lock gates. First known as Topsham Sluice, it later changed its name to Trenchard's Sluice after its keeper. The increased depth of this improved waterway enabled larger ships to reach Exeter.

In 1698, the city chamber had to grapple with the question of what to do with the canal. Trade had increased since the Civil War, woollen goods were again being carried eastwards and westwards, and foreign merchants had settled in Exeter. Many of those employed in the wool trade were descendants of French and Dutch Huguenots, who had fled to England to escape persecution. This was particularly the case in 1572, after the St Bartholomew's Day massacre.

At St Olave's Church, at the top of Fore Street, names of French origin can be seen in memorials and in the window glass. The church was given over to the French Huguenots in 1686, and they conducted their services in French here for many years. Eventually their families became assimilated and the English language prevailed.

In the eighteenth century, further work was completed on the canal, increasing its depth to ten feet and width to fifty. This meant that coasters and other sea-going ships of the age could travel along it. The three old lock gates were removed and replaced by Double Locks, and the 'new' pair of flood gates of the King's Arms Sluice were installed. During the reign of James I, the King's arms were displayed to the right of the lock gates between the river and the canal. This gave notice to shipping that duty would have to be paid on goods passing this point. The sluice gates were necessary to protect the canal when the river was in flood. There were occasions when ships could come up only to this point and then had to wait for the river level to drop.

In 1827, the canal was extended again – to Turf, near Powderham, the home of the Courtenays. Three years later the City Basin was constructed, because the natural impediments in the river bed prevented large ships from reaching the Quay. These works were engineered by the famous James Green, who used to live in what is now the Imperial Hotel in Exeter.

The Basin opened for business on 29 September 1830. The city's five large lighters, decorated with bunting and garlands and filled with ladies and gentlemen, proceeded down to Double Locks and sailed slowly back. Ensconced in a small barge, the band played to entertain the dignitaries and the hundreds of spectators who lined the banks of the enlarged canal. The Cathedral bells rang out and the whole fleet making the maiden journey was started with the firing of a cannon. The Exeter Ship Canal, the only one of its type in Devon, was now the 100 feet wide, 14 feet deep and $5\frac{1}{4}$ miles long waterway which we see today. From now on, traffic on the canal was able to load and unload cargo irrespective of the state of the river.

The canal continued to prosper until 1844, when the railways came to Exeter. This new and revolutionary form of transport took away most of the sea-going trade. However, in spite of this, 275 boats were still using the canal at the turn of the century.

Trade declined during the First World War. The horse used for towing barges was removed from its stable at Turf and restabled at Exeter. Steam vessels came up the canal but the wash from the propellers caused havoc to its banks. The fall in traffic was also partly due to silting up of the canal, an on-going problem for the authorities, who purchased yet another new dredger.

Shipping and trade began to pick up again in the 1930s, the main imports being oil, coal, timber, cement and sugar. However, the outbreak of the Second World War in 1939 curtailed trade, except for petrol. Horse towage ceased altogether. Several bombs fell near the canal, and there was a direct hit on the Basin.

Traffic began slowly to increase during the 1950s, but severe weather in 1963 froze the canal for over a month, and traffic slackened off again. Over its commercial lifetime, many things seemed to go against the smooth running of this waterway.

As stated earlier, the largest ship to use it was the National Benzole tanker *Ben Johnson*, whilst the last regular trader was the oil tanker *Esso Jersey*. Commercial trade ceased in 1972, when the Esso Depot closed and the *Esso Jersey* was switched to coastal work.

The Dutch coaster *Jenco* made occasional visits to the Basin to bring timber for Gabriel Wade and English Ltd.

Soon after the Maritime Museum opened in 1969, a replica of the Hudson Bay Company's first ship paid a visit to Exeter. This was the 50-ton ketch *Nonsuch*, built at Appledore in North Devon to celebrate the company's tercentenary; it sailed up the canal to the Quay and moored there for five days.

The sludge boat used to make regular trips to the sea from the sewage works at Countess Wear.

The canal was in constant need of dredging and yet another new dredger was bought in 1971. A considerable amount of money was spent to dredge the Quay so that the *Onedin Line* schooner *Charlotte Rhodes* could tie up there whilst filming took place.

If you cross the bridge by the King's Arms sluice, and look across the river, you can see the Royal West of England School for the Deaf on the hillside. An article in *Trewman's Flying Post*, 30 March 1826, invited gentlemen of the county to meet to see if it would be feasible to establish a school for the deaf, of the counties of Devon and Cornwall, in or near Exeter. It stated that a private school had been performing this function for a few years but, in order to enlarge it, patronage was needed. If interested, gentlemen could form a committee to submit plans to the public.

The article was written by Mrs Hippisley Tuckfield, who, with her friend Miss Grace Fursdon, was amazed by the progress of a farm labourer's deaf child living at Fursdon, near Bickleigh.

Mrs Tuckfield visited a deaf institution in Paris, and was so impressed with the standard of education that, when she returned, she sought out two more children and housed and educated them at Little Fulford, now Shobrooke Park. The gentlemen of the county then saw the need to establish an institution for the deaf in Exeter.

A meeting was held in what is now the Royal Clarence Hotel and it was decided that such an establishment should be founded for 'the deaf and not deficient in intellect'. Families would have to pay a sum of not less than three shillings a week towards maintenance, and proper clothes had to be provided. In 1827, staff were appointed, a house in 'Alphington Causeway' was rented, and six 'foundation pupils' were admitted.

The master was able to accept private pupils at a charge of seven shillings a week and within a few months the school had 26 pupils. It was obvious that larger premises were needed; later in 1827, the governors purchased three and a quarter acres of land from William Hooper, a local builder. Buildings were erected on the chosen site in Topsham Road. The children and staff moved into their new school after Christmas. This building was in continuous use until 1969. Some parents were unable to find the fees and were reluctant to ask for support, but Mrs Tuckfield understood their attitude and arranged a bazaar, which raised £202 and saved the day. In 1829 she established a 'Bazaar Fund', which was renamed The Samaritan Fund in 1886, to provide funds for needy families.

In those formative years, practical subjects such as tailoring, printing, woodwork, carving and shoe-making were introduced to ensure that not only academic work was covered. Children were encouraged to remain at school until eighteen years old, although the starting age was still only ten. The establishment continued to prosper, and many ex-pupils returned to visit, having secured good, well-paid jobs.

By 1870 there was a network of schools for deaf children throughout the United Kingdom.

In 1913, a new wing was completed, comprising six classrooms, a sick bay and a laundry. This establishment was renamed 'The Royal West of England Residential School for the Deaf' in 1938. The following year, 52 boys from London were evacuated to the school.

When Exeter was bombed on 2 May 1942, the buildings were badly damaged but because of the sensible sleeping arrangements – children on the ground floor – there were no casualties. They were sent home, returning on 14 July when the buildings were fit for use again.

Extra land was purchased in 1947 and by 1951 a building to accommodate nursery children was completed. It was another ten years before a second teaching building, the Daw Block, was opened. In 1963, the Department of Education and Science recommended that it was no longer viable to modernise the buildings, and suggested that new ones should be constructed. A four-year project began in 1967 to address this. The Department gave most of the cost of £646,000. The Daw Block was converted into practical rooms and the gym and swimming bath were modernised. Two new sick bays, complete with surgeries, were added.

In the 1970s, the school provided a comprehensive, inter-denominational education for nursery, first, middle and secondary stages for partially hearing and deaf children. Arrangements were also made to integrate children to Exeter College and Bicton; suitable candidates were prepared for entrance exams to academically selective schools and further education colleges for the deaf.

The school, still flourishing, is a credit to Mrs Hippisley Tuckfield's dreams and efforts all those years ago.

Before continuing our walk between the river and the canal, we can take another look across the river to spy the tall spire of St Leonard's Church.

The first church on this site was built by either Richard de Redvers, the first Earl of Devon, or his son Baldwin, some time after the recording of the Domesday Book. This church was replaced in 1831, but the new one was found to be structurally unsound so was demolished. In 1876 it was replaced by the Victorian Gothic Revival building we now see on the skyline. The 145-foot-high spire was the gift of Mrs Miles of Dix's Field, in memory of her husband. She also built the Clock Tower and horse troughs in Queen Street as a memorial to him, as he was so fond of horses.

We now find ourselves beside a wide, low area partly filled with water, its long high concrete wall dividing it from the river. Whenever I walk past here there is always a line of birds perched along the top of the wall. This is the start of a flood relief channel, which is only in use when the river can no longer cope with its flow.

Much new building has taken place on the St Thomas bank of the Exeter Canal.

We now make our way over a concrete bridge, which spans this 'overflow' channel. We soon arrive at the suspension bridge, which spans the river.

This footbridge was built in the 1930s to allow people from the recently-built Burnthouse Lane estate to get to work more easily, if they worked to the west of the river

and canal. A plaque on the northern end of the bridge gives details of its construction. Many have suggested that it should have a name, and the Match Factory Bridge would seem to be the obvious choice.

To our left is a splendid view of Trew's Weir, and beyond to the city. This weir was originally constructed of stakes and brushwood and called St Leonard's Weir.

Having crossed the bridge, we see on the right an open park. This is Belle Isle Park, where the City Council once raised plants for the city's flowerbeds. Before that it was the site of a sewage works.

To our left is the Match Factory, an important example of industrial architecture. There is no record that matches were ever made here, but I have heard that a former owner of the building collected signs, and when he obtained a sign saying 'Match Factory' he erected it on his property. We do know that in the 1850s it was a flax mill, and the area to the right of it was a retting pond, for soaking the flax. Its history suggests it was also a place where paper bags were made. When this industry ceased, the buildings appear to have been used as a stable.

Last of all, it became a social club for the workers of the almost adjacent Pitts' paper mill.

We walk along the path and, where it meets another path, turn left. To our right there is a large white house behind a wall, which was where the Pitts family once lived, but Mrs Pitts has now sold it. Next to it is a long, three-storey building made of local Heavitree stone; this was the paper mill, now converted into apartments.

The site has a long history. In 1793, a lease was given to R. Tipping to build a mill in a field by Trew's Weir. This was not to be used for fulling cloth or grinding grain, so it became a cotton mill employing about 300 men. It closed in 1812, and the building became tenements. At that time John Heathcote, who had been driven out of Loughborough, inspected it, but in the end he decided to set up his lace business in Tiverton. That town remains ever grateful.

In 1834, the building was converted into a paper mill; it became the property of John Pitts and Sons in 1907. At one time paper manufactured here was used for the tickets issued on the London Underground. The changing face of paper manufacture saw the demise of this concern, and a great many others like it, in the second half of the 20th century.

A little further on we see, on the right, a modern reproduction of an old mill-race. Beyond this, also to our right, there is a large area of land which at one time belonged to the mill. Now it is developed with tall, quality, red-brick houses and apartments.

We soon pass the Port Royal Inn. A high yellowish stone wall interspersed with some Heavitree stones lies to our right just beyond it. Behind this and much higher up the hill is the house called Larkbeare, the residence of judges when the courts are in session at Rougemont Castle. Consequently it's always known as 'Judges' Lodgings'.

Until earlier in this century, the riverside between the flats and Larkbeare was known as St Leonard's Quay; its main use was for loading ballast, mainly scrap metal, for departing traffic.

We have now reached the end of Colleton Hill, a fairly short steep street, which has a terrace of cottages along the right hand side of it. They were once occupied by people who worked in the lime kilns situated at the end of this hill. Boats brought stone chippings from Torbay and coal from South Wales to the area and the two, placed in alternating layers, were burnt together to make quicklime for agricultural use and to whitewash cottages.

Colleton Hill leads to Colleton Crescent and Melbourne Street, and its houses present a really bright and cheerful appearance.

To conclude our walk, all we have to do is remain on the level, continue beside the river, and we will arrive back at Exeter's historic quayside area.